पत्नी Patnee
Wife

In the eyes of husband

R.N. Kogata • Lalita Kogata

D.K. Printworld (P) Ltd.
New Delhi

Cataloging in Publication Data — DK
[Courtesy: D.K. Agencies (P) Ltd. <docinfo@dkagencies.com>]

Kogata, R. N. (Ram Narayan), 1964–
Patnee = Wife : in the eyes of husband /
R.N. Kogata, Lalita Kogata.
p. cm.
English and Hindi.
ISBN 13: 9788124604847
ISBN 10: 8124604843

1. Wives — Prayers and devotions. 2. Man-woman relationships in art. 3. Spouses in art. 4. Love in art. 5. Parvati (Hindu deity) — Art. 6. Siva (Hindu deity) — Art. 7. Art, Hindu. I. Kogata, Lalita, 1965–, joint author. II. Title. III. Title: Wife : in the eyes of husband.

DDC 306.872 22

First Published in India, 2009
ISBN 13: 978-81-246-0484-7
ISBN 10: 81-246-0484-3

A Creation of:
Mr. R.N. Kogata
Mrs. Lalita Kogata
608, Hiran Magari, Sector-11, Udaipur - India
Phone : +91-94141-58870
devkush@rediffmail.com

Published and printed by:
D.K. Printworld (P) Ltd.
'Sri Kunj' F-52, Bali Nagar
Ramesh Nagar Metro Stn., New Delhi - 110015
Phs.: 011-2545 3975, 2546 6019
Fax: 011-2546 5926
Email: dkprintworld@vsnl.net
Web: www.dkprintworld.com

पत्नी Patnee Wife

In the eyes of husband

सा भार्या या गृहे दक्षा सा भार्या या प्रियंवदा।
सा भार्या या पतिप्राणा सा भार्या या प्रजावती॥

— चाणक्य राजनीतिशास्त्र, 1.28

पत्नी वह है जो गृह कार्य में दक्ष हो, प्रियभाषिणी हो, पति परायणा हो और सन्तति वाली हो।

A good wife is she who is well-versed in domestic chores, is of sweet speech, is devoted to her husband, and is blessed with children.

॥ ॐ गं गणपतये नमः ॥

Preface

Most people today lack a basic understanding of what is marriage and also the importance of wife, who is the centre of gravity for any house. As the time passes after marriage, the life of most of the people becomes routine and most men take their wives for granted without realizing the hard work and sacrifice she has done for the family. In fact, a woman plays a vital role in the family and keeps the family knit together.

A wife is normally a lifetime companion at times of prosperity, distress, famine, subduing of enemies and in a graveyard, whereas other relatives may not always remain with you. A wife always wishes for her husband's good only even if the husband is not good, and serves him with love and affection and therefore such wives are called *Pativrataa,* devoted to the husband.

It is said, respect your wife and make every effort to keep her happy; for a good wife and health are a man's best wealth.

Fortitude, Courage, Tolerance, Flexibility, Patience, Firmness, Sacrifice, Blessings, Love, Affection, Faith, Belief, Kindness, Mercy and nearly every other brave aspect of human soul is possessed by a woman, who has many forms — a mother, a wife, a sister, a daughter and so on. A woman can be very humble, loving, sacrificing, understanding and supporting to you if respected, but can also take the form of Goddess Durga, Kali and Chandi, if she is not happy and satisfied and not respected. Wife gives you the power and patience of fighting with all the problems of the world. The man should become his wife's cheerleader and should not become a social butterfly but should be really supportive to the wife.

For the kind of role a wife plays in the life of a man and his whole family, her debt can only be paid back by becoming part of her dreams, becoming her friend, making her your world, avoiding inhibitions coming in the way, talking together, walking together, thinking together, understanding, listening to her patiently, becoming her sounding board, realize her hard work and sacrifice, encouraging her and not nagging, respecting and allowing her to fulfill her wishes, paying her compliments, appreciating her work, gestures and ideas, doing everything for her with inner joy of giving, admitting your mistakes gracefully, giving her due time, and so on.

By the poem presented in the book, we are not only reminding the male community about the importance of wife but also about the indispensable place she occupies in each and every family. This book is a small attempt by us to express our respect and gratitude towards all the wives of the world, without whom the families would lose not only the peace, happiness and harmony but also social standing, confidence and respect.

We are grateful to His Highness Shreeji Arvind Singh Mewar for his worthy guidance from time to time. We prostrate before our parents Shri Bhairav Lal Kogata and Smt Kanchan Devi Kogata and Prof K.M. Nuwal and Smt Kamla Devi Nuwal and all our family members for their beloved blessings, without which we would not have reached this stage.

R.N. Kogata
Lalita Kogata

Importance of Wife

iyam sita mama sutaa
sahadharma caree tava ।
prateeccha cainaam badramte
paanim grihneesva paaninaa ।
pativrataa mahaa bhaaga
caaya ivaanugathaa sataa ।।

Reciting this verse King Janaka of Mithila gave away his daughter Sita to Rama in marriage. The meaning of this verse is:

> Here is my daughter Sita. She will accompany you in your path of *dharma*. Hold her hand, let all auspiciousness come to you, Rama. She will protect her chastity, earn all virtues, and will follow you like your shadow. She will never leave you.

From this we see that chastity is the most important characteristic of a wife.

When Sita is in the Ashokavana, Ravana goes to beg of her to become his queen. To his entreaties Sita replies:

> O evil man! I have married Rama and will never leave him. Having held his hands, I will never touch another man's hand. Just as Veda belongs to a *brahmachari*, I belong to Rama only. If anyone sees me with evil intention, with my virtue I will burn him to ashes.

In both Hindu and Christian scriptures, the story about the origin of woman appears to be similar. It is stated in *Manusmriti* (1.32), that Brahma divided his own body into two and made one part male and the other part female. The male embraced the female from which union was born the Viraat Purusha.

In the book of Genesis in the Bible, the origin of the first woman is given. God created Adam as the first man. God caused a deep sleep to fall upon Adam. Then he took a rib from Adam, made a woman with it, and gave that woman, who was called Eve, to Adam as wife.

According to Manu it is the duty of the husband to protect his wife, and it is the duty of the wife to obey her husband.

During their forest life Rama and Sita reached the hermitage of sage Atri, and the sage and his wife Anusuya treated the guests sumptuously. Atri told Rama that Anusuya's *tapas shakti* caused rain to fall and Ganga to flow again after a ten-year period of famine. Anusuya taught Sita that absolute service to husband is the greatest *tapas* ordained to women.

According to the Puranas, Arundhati outshone all other chaste women in devotion to her husband, sage Vasishta. She owed her great power to her chastity and service of her husband. During the marriage ceremony, the husband shows his wife the Arundhati star in the Saptarshimandala, which symbolically means that the wife should possess all the good characters which Arundhati possessed.

In Hindu iconography, Shiva has given his left half to his consort Uma or Parvati. In Shiva temples we find the idol of

Ardhanarishvara with the right half showing Shiva's form and the left Devi's form. This also shows that wife is one half of the husband, i.e. *ardhaangini*. We normally call the wife the "better half."

The *Arthashaastra*, in many ways more liberal than the religious text books, lays down quite stringent rules for the punishment of immodest wives. According to *Arthashaastra* a modest wife is one who does not take part in games, or drinks, against her husband's wishes; does not leave home without his permission; does not leave the house while her husband is asleep or drunk; and does not converse with a man facetiously in secret.

Manusmriti (chapter V), states:

> She (a wife) should always be cheerful, and skilful in her domestic duties, with her household vessels well cleansed and her hand tight on the purse-strings. . . .
>
> Though he be uncouth and prone to pleasure, though he has no good points at all, the virtuous wife should ever worship her lord as a god.

Passages of this type are frequent in literature and stories of obedient and faithful wives are numerous. The great models of Indian womanhood or wifehood are Sita who faithfully followed her husband Rama into exile and endured great hardships for his sake, and Savitri, who followed her husband Satyavan when he was being carried away by the death-god Yama, and so impressed the god with her loyalty that he released her lord.

The *Mahabharata* says:

> The wife is half the man, the best of friends, the root of the three ends of life, and of all that will help him in the other world.
>
> With a wife a man does mighty deeds . . . with a wife a man finds courage. A wife is the safest refuge. . . .
>
> A man aflame with sorrow in his soul, or sick with disease, finds comfort in his wife, as a man parched with heat finds relief in water.
>
> Even a man in the grip of rage will not be harsh to a woman, remembering that on her depend the joys of love, happiness, and virtue.
>
> For woman is the everlasting field, in which the Self is born.

Thus we find that a wife is given lot of respect in our society provided she is virtuous, serves her husband and his family with sincerity, guides her husband properly in the path of *dharma*, and begets children and rears them to become noble persons in life. All these will be possible only it the wife enacts these roles with diligence at her rightful place in the world stage, i.e. her home. Of course, times have changed a lot and more and more women, who are wives as well, are competing with men and are doing all sorts of jobs outside of their homes. Nevertheless, the wives should remember that to be chaste and virtuous is within their control, and only good character and sincere service can earn them the respect they deserve in the society, as "friend, philosopher and guide."

तू मेरी शर्म है, हया है, संस्कार है।
तू ही मेरा पहला और आखिरी प्यार है।।

पत्नी
Patnee
Wife

You are my modesty, my bashfulness, my embellishment.
You are the first and the last love of my life.

पत्नी
Patnee
Wife

तू मेरी नम्रता है, समझ है, सहिष्णुता है।
बड़ों के आशीर्वाद से तू मेरी परिणिता है।।

You are my politeness, my understanding, my tolerance.
You are my life partner with the blessings of elders.

तू मेरा धैर्य है, धीरज है, सांत्वना है।
तेरे आने से महका मेरा अंगना है।।

पत्नी
Patnee
W i f e

You are my patience, my tolerance, my solace.
Your entry has made my home odorous.

तू मेरा मन है, आत्मा है, भावना है।
तू है तो जिंदगी में सारी संभावना है।।

पत्नी
Patnee
Wife

You are my heart, my soul, my emotions.
Everything is possible for me with your presence.

तू मेरा सुख है, शांति है, संतोष है।
तेरा साथ है तो जिंदगी में जोश है।।

पत्नी
Patnee
wife

You are my happiness, my peace, my contentment.
Your company with me creates life's real excitement.

तू मेरा न्याय है, निर्णय है, हल है।
तेरी उपस्थिति मेरे बाजुओं का बल है।।

पत्नी
Patnee
Wife

You are my justice, my decision, my solution.
Your presence improves and maintains power in my arms.

तू मेरी उमंग है, उत्साह है, जोश है।
तेरे बिन ये जिंदगी खानाबदोश है।।

पत्नी Patnee Wife

You are my enthusiasm, my encouragement, my excitement.
Life is vagabond without your presence.

पत्नी
Patnee
Wife

तू मेरी दोस्ती है, प्यार है, मोहब्बत है।
तूने अपने कामों से बढ़ाई घर की इज्जत है।।

You are my friendship, my love, my affection.
You have increased the respect of the family by your work.

तू मेरी तल्लीनता है, सम्मोहन है, तन्मयता है।
तेरे होने से ये मकान घर बनता है।।

पत्नी
Patnee
Wife

You are my fascination, my hypnotism, my concentration.
The house is converted to home by your presence.

तू मेरा साहस है, हिम्मत है, हौंसला है।
तेरे होने से ही ये दीवारें प्यार का घौंसला है।।

You are my fortitude, my courage, my intrepidity.
These walls are snug of love only because of your availability.

तू मेरा जादू है, जुनून है, चमत्कार है।
तू ही मेरे बच्चों का स्नेह और दुलार है।।

पत्नी Patnee Wife

You are my magic, my miracle, my passion.
You are the love and affection of our children.

तू मेरा सुर है, नृत्य है, ताल है।
तेरी संभाल से ये परिवार मालामाल है।।

पत्नी
Patnee
Wife

You are my tune, my dance, my rhythm.
The family is rich with your care.

तू मेरा ज्ञान है, बुद्धि है, सृजनता है।
तेरे दिये संस्कारों से ही घर बनता है।।

पत्नी
Patnee
Wife

You are my knowledge, my creativity, my wisdom.
The home is made by the gift of your ornamentation.

पत्नी
Patnee
Wife

तू मेरा भोलापन है, भलाई है, परोपकार है।
तेरी ये खूबियां ही मेरा संसार है।।

You are my innocence, my well being, my benevolence.
The whole world is made for me by presence of these characteristics.

तू मेरी दीप्ति है, रंग है, चमक है।
तेरा दुपट्टा जैसे बागों में फूलों की महक है।।

पत्नी
Patnee
Wife

You are my color, my flash, my illumination.
Your scarf is like fragrance of flower in garden.

तू मेरा अनुभव है, भरोसा है, विश्वास है।
तेरा स्थान मेरे जीवन में बहुत खास है।।

पत्नी
Patnee
Wife

You are my experience, my dependence, my confidence.
Your place in my life has much of importance.

तू मेरी पार्वती है, राधा है, सीता है।
तू ही तो रामायण, कुरान और गीता है।।

पत्नी Patnee Wife

You are my Paarvati, my Radha, my Sita.
You only are the Ramayan, Kuran and Geeta.

तू मेरा छन्द है, कविता है, दोहा है।
तेरी सादगी ने मेरा मन मोहा है।।

पत्नी
Patnee
Wife

You are my stanza, my poem, my couplet.
Your simplicity has attracted my heart.

तू मेरी पृथ्वी है, आसमान है, सृष्टि है।
तू मेरे प्यारे से प्यार की अभिव्यक्ति है।।

पत्नी
Patnee
Wife

You are my earth, my ether, my universe.
You are the expression of my lovely love.

तू मेरी लक्ष्मी है, तुलसी है, सरस्वती है।
तेरे प्यार से मेरे जीवन की नदी बहती है।।

पत्नी
Patnee
wife

You are my Laxmi, my Tulsi, my Saraswati.
My life's river flows only with your love.

तू मेरा दर्शन है, चिंतन है, मनन है।
तू ही मेरी भावनाओं का सुन्दर सा दर्पण है।।

पत्नी
Patnee
Wife

You are my philosophy, my meditation, my reflections.
You are the beautiful mirror of my emotions.

तू मेरा संतुलन है, ऊँचाई है, शिखर है।
तेरे दिल में सबकी जगह जैसे सागर है।।

पत्नी
Patnee
Wife

You are my balance, my height, my crown.
Your heart has as big a place for everyone as sea as it is shown.

तू मेरी नींद है, आराम है, सुकून है।
तेरे सहयोग से ही सफलता का जुनून है।।

पत्नी
Patnee
Wife

You are my sleep, my rest, my comfort.
Your co-operation only creates passion of success.

तू मेरी नदी है, सागर है, झरना है।
जीवन के सारे काम तेरे संग करना है।।

Patnee पत्नी
Wife

You are my river, my sea, my water fall.
Life desires to complete with you its work all.

तू मेरा पर्व है, त्यौहार है, चारों धाम है।
तेरे हाथों से ही बनते मेरे सारे काम है।।

पत्नी Patnee Wife

You are my festival, my four holy places, my occasions.
All my works are successful when done with your hands.

तू मेरा नशा है, सुरूर है, सपना है।
तेरा साथ है तो दुनियाँ में सब अपना है।।

पत्नी
Patnee
Wife

You are my over joy, my dream, my intoxication.
If you are with me, everything in the world looks in perfection.

तू मेरी स्थिरता है, शक्ति है, भक्ति है।
तू साथ है तो मेरी हार नहीं हो सकती है।।

पत्नी Patnee Wife

You are my stability, my veneration, my power.
I cannot lose anything, if I have the companion's love shower.

तू मेरी हवा है, प्रकाश है, धूप है।
तू मेरे मन की ऊँचाईयों का स्तूप है।।

पत्नी
Patnee
W i f e

You are my wind, my sunlight, my light.
You are the Buddhistic tope of my heart's heights.

पत्नी
Patnee
Wife

अब तो समझ गई हो कि मेरा सब कुछ तू ही है।
जिंदगी तेरे बिन बस मर जाना यूं ही है।।
इसलिये खयाले बिछड़ना भी मन में आ नहीं सकता।
तुझे कोई भी तकलीफ़ हो, ये मन को भा नहीं सकता।।
इसलिये भगवान से प्रार्थना यही है।
तेरा मेरा साथ हमेशा रहे, यही बिल्कुल सही है।

You must have understood that you are every thing for me in my life.
Life without you is like dieing without cause.
So even the thought of separation cannot come to my heart.
You have any problem, my heart can never accept.
Therefore, I only pray to God
that the best thing for us is to continue living together forever.

Even in the deep forest, the wife is the refreshment
and solace of her roaming husband.

पत्नी Patnee Wife

He, who has a wife, is trusted by all.
The wife, therefore, is man's great means of salvation.